Mini-Moments
for
Christmas

Mini-Moments for Christmas

by Robert Strand

New Leaf Press

First printing: July 1996
Third printing: September 2004

ISBN: 0-89221-330-2
Library of Congress Catalog No. 96-69685

Printed in the United States of America.

Please visit our website for other great titles:
www.newleafpress.net

For information regarding author interviews, please contact the
publicity department at (870) 438-5288.

Presented to:

_____

Presented by:

_____

Date:

_____

That Special Name

When I was a child, the Christmas season seemed to last only about ten days but now it seems that merchants are stretching it from Labor Day to New Year's. Think back to summer: Quick, when did your first Christmas catalog arrive? Ours came sometime in late July.

There is no other festive occasion that enjoys such expansion. George Washington's birthday still occupies one day; the dimensions of Independence Day are firmly fixed to one day only; Armistice Day is almost forgotten; Labor Day gets little more than a passing thought.

BUT CHRISTMAS GETS BIGGER EVERY YEAR! WHY? From the viewpoint of business, the name of Jesus triggers the biggest buying spree of the year. But beyond the commercial appeal, I believe it to be a part of our search for happiness, the search for meaning, the hope of a new start, and peace in our homes. It's all part of an inner cry for God!

This Christmas season will be only as
meaningful as we make it.

Therefore God exalted Him to the highest place and gave
Him the name that is above every name, that at the name of
Jesus every knee should bow, in heaven and on earth
and under the earth, and every tongue confess that Jesus
Christ is Lord, to the glory of God the Father
(Phil. 2:9–11).

Fed Up with Christmas

I'm fed up with Christmas! Now that sounds pretty stupid coming from a man who goes to church as often as he can and who thinks that the Christ born at Christmas is the greatest gift ever given!

What I mean is that I'm fed up with what a lot of us are doing with Christmas. We have gone crazy and almost shot it to pieces. Last year, I read about a bunch of guys who spent Christmas Eve in a night club and how they chipped in to buy a poor kid some toys. They probably spent ten times as much on drinks as on toys. They went home to sleep it off, happy that they'd kept the Christmas spirit.

Maybe I'm getting soft in the head or heart. Christmas is more than sentimental stories. It's about the Bethlehem Baby! When you think about it . . . there's only ONE Christmas story!

Christmas is not just a day, an event to be
observed and speedily forgotten. It is a spirit
which should permeate every part of our lives.

(William Parks)

The virgin will be with child and will give birth
to a son, and they will call him Immanuel"
— which means, "God with us"

(Matt. 1:23).

Ah! dearest Jesus, Holy Child,
Make thee a bed, soft, undefiled,
Within my heart, that it may be
A quiet chamber kept for thee.

Martin Luther (1483–1546)

Overlooked

A Sunday school class made up of three and four year olds was part of the annual church Christmas program. They had given their little recitations and sung their songs and were now on their way down from the platform. On their way off stage, they passed by the place where the pastor was sitting. As each little one passed, he smiled, or patted them on the head and made some remark about their participation. Somehow he missed one little boy . . . this little guy burst into tears, broke from his place in the line, and ran for his mother. As she picked him up, between his sobs he was heard to say, "God didn't smile at me."

We smile at that, childish simplicity. But don't all of us, inwardly, long for the smile of God as desperately as that little child longed for his pastor's approval smile?

It is good to be children sometimes, and never
better than at Christmas, when its mighty
founder was a child himself.

(Charles Dickens)

For unto us a child is born, to us a Son is given,
and the government will be on His shoulders.
And He will be called Wonderful Counselor, Mighty God,
Everlasting Father, Prince of Peace
(Isa. 9:6).

The First U.S. Christmas

Think back with me to December 25, 1776. Destiny was in the making. We were at war for our freedom from the British who held the cities, leaving our troops in the cold and snow.

That night the town of Trenton, New Jersey, was ablaze with light and celebrations. Houses were filled with professional German troops and nobody cared about George Washington and his ragged army. To these professionals, Washington's troops were nothing but a rabble in arms. But Washington was on the move, he crossed the Delaware. It was a clean plan. He pulled his guns and men up that bank . . . then attacked! He drove Colonel Ralls and his men into the cold. It was the battle which turned the war. Before he finished, every post in the Delaware River territory had been cleared of the enemy.

So it was that very first Christmas. Christmas heralded the end for the forces of hell. Christmas Day meant war . . . the birth of Jesus brings deliverance for the captives.

The miracle of Christmas is that a baby
can be so decisive.

The Spirit of the Lord is on Me, because he has
anointed Me to preach good news to the poor.
He has sent Me to proclaim freedom for the prisoner
and recovery of sight for the blind, to release
the oppressed, to proclaim the year of the Lord's favor
(Luke 4:18–19).

The Hallelujah Chorus

I've been accused of not being such a hot musician, but that doesn't keep me from enjoying great music. One of my absolute favorites is to hear Handel's "Hallelujah Chorus" performed at Christmas. A rousing tribute of praise that is unexcelled in our music.

Did you know that Handel sketched and scored the entire composition in an incredible 21 days? And when the oratorio was performed for the first time before the king, as he heard those mighty hallelujahs . . . he was so moved he stood to his feet, meaning the entire crowd of people had to follow suit. Someone has suggested that the king was on his way to the bathroom. If so, it must have surprised him to see the entire audience ready to join him. Well . . . whatever, contemporary audiences still rise when that magnificent chorus is reached. I stand, too, but

have a hard time restraining myself from also raising my arms and joining with them! Hallelujah is a Hebrew word meaning PRAISE THE LORD!

Christmas is the time in which all of us should give praise to the Lord . . . which He is deemed worthy to receive.

"Amen, Hallelujah!"
Then a voice came from the throne saying:
"Praise our God, all you His servants, you who fear Him,
both small and great!"
(Rev. 19:4–5).

When the angels had left them and gone into heaven, the shepherds said to one another, "Let's go to Bethlehem and see this thing that has happened, which the Lord has told us about"
(Luke 2:15).

The Perfect Gift That Fits Everybody

Are you still looking for that exactly just right gift to give this Christmas season? Here's one that is easy to find, inexpensive, non-fattening, and fits all sizes: HUGGING! Yes, you are reading this right, hugging! Hugging has been found to be healthy because it helps the body's immune system, it cures depression, it reduces stress, it induces sleep, it's invigorating, it's rejuvenating, it has no unpleasant side effects, anyone can apply it, it is unbreakable, and it works like a miracle drug!

Not only that, HUGGING is all natural . . . it is organic, naturally sweet, no preservatives, no pesticides, no artificial ingredients, and 100 percent wholesome! HUGGING is practically perfect . . . no movable parts, no batteries to wear out, no periodic check-ups, low energy yield, no assembly required, and always . . . fully returnable! Try it! You might be really surprised!

Perhaps the best Yuletide decorations are to
be wreathed in smiles and wrapped in hugs.

Whoever does not love does not know God, because
God is love. This is how God showed his love among us:
He sent His one and only Son into the world that
we might live through him

(1 John 4:8–9).

A Child's Perspective

The first graders at an Episcopal Sunday school in San Diego were told to draw on paper their conceptions of the "flight into Egypt" by Mary, Joseph, and the baby Jesus. One little girl turned in a picture of an airplane with three people in the back, all with halos, and a fourth up front without one. Perplexed about the picture, the teacher asked the little girl to explain.

"Oh," replied the youngster, "that's Mary, Joseph, and the baby Jesus in the back."

The teacher went on, "And what about the fourth person?"

"That," said the little girl with emphasis, "is Pontius, the pilot!"

Children are wonderful! The wonder and magic of this season is special to them or it should be. Perhaps, if you have kids or know kids you could encourage them this season with the real story of Christmas. Help them to see beyond the glitz and gift-giving to the real reason for this season.

At Christmas . . . too many parents will spend
more money on their kids than they did on
their honeymoon which started it all.

When Jesus saw this, he was indignant.

He said to them, "Let the little children come to me,

and do not hinder them, for the kingdom of God

belongs to such as these"

(Mark 10:14).

Murphy's Holiday Laws

Murphy has done it again! Here's an updated version of "Murphy's Holiday Laws" from the same people who brought you the original, "If anything can go wrong it will," Murphy's Law. Hold on, because here we go:

* The time it takes to find a parking space is inversely proportional to the amount of time you have to spend.

* The more expensive a breakable gift is, the better your chances of dropping it.

* The other check-out line always moves faster.

* Unassembled toys will have twice as many screws as you expect and some will always be left over, making you wonder what's left out.

And come to think of it . . . Murphy might have been an optimist! I'm for living through this season without letting the little inconveniences of this celebration season get to any of us.

The Christmas season reminds us that a
demonstration of religion is always much
better than a definition of it
. . . especially in front of the kids.

Jesus looked at them and said, "With man this is impossible,

but not with God; all things are possible with God"

(Mark 10:27).

*Are you willing to stoop down and consider the
needs and desires of little children; to remember the
weaknesses and loneliness of people who are growing
old; to stop asking how much your friends love you, and
to ask yourself whether you love them enough; to bear
in mind the things that other people have to bear on
their hearts; to trim your lamp so that it will give more
light and less smoke, and to carry it in front so that your
shadow will fall behind you; to make a grave for your
ugly thoughts and a garden for your kindly feelings,
with the gate open? Are you willing to do these things
for a day? Then you are ready to keep Christmas!*

Henry Van Dyke (1852–1933)

Xmas or Christmas?

It's not simply the holiday season, but the colloquial "XMAS" which has been singled out as one example of how the holiday has become commercialized and robbed of its religious content. The "X" in "Xmas" is actually the descendent of the Greek language equivalent of "Ch" as in "Christos" which means "Christ." The letter "X" has stood for Christ since at least A.D. 1100, and the term "Xmas" was first used in the year A.D. 1551. Greek language expert Eric Partridge points out that the abbreviation for Christianity is "Xianity."

Many people dislike "Xmas" for any usage because of its supposed crassness. The *New York Times Manual of Style and Usage* offers this simple recommendation for when "Xmas" is acceptable: "Never use."

And so now you know. . . .

Christmas is the season when everybody
wants his or her past forgotten
and the present remembered.

He came to that which was his own,

but his own did not receive him. Yet to all

who received him, to those who believed in his name,

he gave the right to become children of God

(John 1:11–12).

Nothing Between

There's an old story about a little ghetto boy whose parents were dead, so he had been left in the care of a drunken aunt, who beat and half-starved him. The greatest delight in his life was to walk the streets during the Christmas season and look at the beautiful, wonderful Christmas toys displayed in the store windows. He knew, however, that these toys were not for him because there was always a glass barrier between.

One day, as he was crossing the street, he was struck by a car and taken to a hospital. It was Christmas week and to his surprise he saw other children playing with toys they had received for Christmas. Soon, he sat up in bed, when, wonder of wonders, on the foot of his bed were a number of toys and presents left for him.

Hardly able to believe his eyes . . . he stretched out his hands and said, "There's no glass between!" Sin is the barrier that Christ removed with His coming to this earth.

Christmas living is the best kind
of Christmas giving.

(Van Dyke)

The Word became flesh and made his dwelling among us.

We have seen his glory, the glory of the One and Only, who

came from the Father, full of grace and truth

(John 1:14).

Give the earth to Christ,
A little boy of heavenly birth,
But far from home today,
Comes down to find His ball, the earth
That sin has cast away.
O comrades, let us one and all
Join in to get Him back His ball.

John Bannister Tabb (1845–1909)

Bethlehem Star

In this particular church it was the night of the annual children's Christmas program. There were little kids everywhere and the excitement was running high. There had been rehearsals with teachers practicing with their little charges. Parents were nervous along with the kids who were also uptight. It came time for the first graders to do their presentation . . . but it didn't quite come out as planned.

Thirteen of them were to walk across the platform, each carrying a letter-bearing placard. All together . . . if they were in correct order and in line . . . they would have spelled:

B-E-T-H-L-E-H-E-M S-T-A-R.

But somehow the "star" carriers got turned around and they went in backward, so to speak, spelling out: "B-E-T-H-L-E-H-E-M R-A-T-S!"

Christmas holidays can mean: anticipations,
preparations, presentations, recreations,
fascinations, prostrations, and recuperations.

"Martha, Martha," the Lord answered, "you are worried
and upset about many things, but only one thing
is needed. Mary has chosen what is better"
(Luke 10:41–42).

Home for Christmas

Orville and Wilbur Wright had tried repeatedly to fly a heavier-than-air craft. Finally, on December 17, 1903, it happened. They managed to fly their plane about 120 feet! They actually flew! Elated, they had done what had never been done by anyone before. They wired a telegram with this news back home to their sister Katherine: "We have actually flown 120 feet. STOP Will be home for Christmas. STOP"

She ran down the street all excited, and shoved the telegram, which was the news scoop of the new century, at the city editor of the local daily paper in Dayton, Ohio. The next day he had headlined the story like this: "LOCAL BICYCLE MERCHANTS TO BE HOME FOR CHRISTMAS!"

Talk about missing it! This Christmas . . . please don't miss the *real story!*

This Christmas, remember . . . God shocked
the world with a baby and not a bomb.

*After the Feast was over, while His parents were
returning home, the boy Jesus stayed behind in Jerusalem,
but they were unaware of it. Thinking He was in their
company, they traveled on for a day. They began looking for
Him among their relatives and friends. When they did not
find Him, they went back . . . to look for Him*
(Luke 2:43–45).

A Gift of Love

One of my favorite Christmas stories has to do with a missionary in Africa. Before Christmas she had been telling the students how Christians, in happiness, gave presents to others on the occasion of Christ's birthday.

A few days later, on Christmas morning, one of these native students brought the missionary a beautiful, lustrous seashell. When asked where he had discovered such an extraordinary shell, he said he had walked many miles to a certain ocean bay, the only spot where such shells could be found.

She exclaimed, "What a beautiful gift! It must have been a real sacrifice for you to have traveled so far to get it."

His eyes brightened as he replied, "Long walk, part of gift!"

Selfishness makes Christmas a burden, but
love makes it a delight.

For God so loved the world that he gave
his one and only Son, that whoever believes in him
shall not perish but have eternal life
(John 3:16).

Neither do people light a lamp and put it under

a bowl. Instead they put it on its stand, and it

gives light to everyone in the house

(Matt. 5:15).

Shopping His Own Way

A little boy about six or seven was lost during the Christmas shopping rush. He was standing in an aisle of a busy department store crying, "I want my mommy . . . I want my mommy." People kept passing by, patting him on the head, attempting to comfort him . . . and handing the unhappy child money — dimes, nickels, quarters, pennies, to keep him quiet and happy as they offered him help, which he refused.

Finally, one of the floor managers came over to him and said, "Son, I have found your mommy. I know where she is. . . ."

The pathetic little guy looked up with tear-stained eyes and said, "So do I . . . now just you keep quiet!"

Talk about children and Christmas and innovation and ingenuity. What fun!

I wish we could put up some of the Christmas
spirit in jars and open a jar of it every month.

(Harlan Miller)

Thus there were fourteen generations in all from Abraham to
David, fourteen from David to the exile to Babylon,
and fourteen from the exile to the Christ

(Matt. 1:17).

God Gets a Perfect Score

A college student who happened to be poorly prepared for an economics exam just before the Christmas vacation, was about to give up in despair when he saw the questions. After a bit of thinking, he decided to try a new tactic in test taking. He wrote in large capitals across the test paper: "Only God knows the answers to these questions. MERRY CHRISTMAS!"

The professor graded the papers, which were handed back after the vacation and wrote this note on the same test paper: "God gets a perfect score . . . you get a zero. HAPPY NEW YEAR!"

All this to say . . . let's not go through another season of Christmas without taking some time to prepare our minds, bodies, and most of all, our souls. Why? It's too easy to lose our way in His season.

For centuries people have kept an
appointment with Christmas. Christmas
means fellowship, feasting, giving, and
receiving, a time of good cheer, home.

(W. J. Ronald Tucker)

While they were there, the time came for the baby to be
born, and she gave birth to her firstborn, a son.
She wrapped him in cloths and placed him in a manger,
because there was no room for them in the inn
(Luke 2:6–7).

Unexpected Gifts

On Christmas Eve Day 1974, four Paris garbage collectors were working along the Avenue Marigny behind the presidential palace quite early in the morning when a policeman stopped their truck. The officer than told them that they were to be the special honored guests for breakfast with the president of France, then Mr. d'Estaing. Talk about a surprise! Oh yes, they were to come just as they were. No, this is not a huge prank, the president sends his invitation, which must not be refused.

They were ushered in to places of honor at the presidential table which was already set. The president visited with them, interested in their work and their living. Then he gave each of them a turkey and gifts for their families and wished them an enjoyable day and season!

One of the happiest joys of Christmas is to give to others who cannot possibly return the favor!

After all, Christmas is but a big
love affair to remove the wrinkles of the year
with kindly remembrances.

(John Wanamaker)

But the angel said to them, "Do not be afraid.
I bring you good news of great joy that will be
for all the people. Today in the town of David a Saviour
has been born to you; He is Christ the Lord"

(Luke 2:10–11).

Christmas is not a date.

It is a state of mind.

Mary Ellen Chase (1887–1973)

Christmas Poetry

That Christmas Day, if you were God,
And that was your Son on that stable sod.
  Wrapped for death with its sin-cursed sting.
  Would you have made the angels sing?
Would you have sent a lovely star
To guide the wise men from afar?
  While weaklings did what haters bid?
  Our loving Heavenly Father did.
On the Calv'ry road, if you were God
And that was your Son 'neath the scouring rod
  Bearing pain and bitter loss
  Would you have nailed Him to the cross?
Would you have let Him suffer so
That sinners might salvation know?
  While this He did their sins to rid?
  Our loving Heavenly Father did.

(Paul Radar)

After a Christmas comes a Lent.

(John Ray: English Proverbs)

He was assigned a grave with the wicked,

and with the rich in His death, though He had done no

violence, nor was any deceit in His mouth

(Isa. 53:9).

His Only Forgotten Son

My five-year-old Stephen was practicing his memory verse for Bible Club — John 3:16, "For God so loved the world that He gave His only *forgotten* Son." My wife laughed as she related this story, and so did I. So writes Stuart M. Pederson of Onida, South Dakota.

Yet, could it be? This little slip of the tongue might be all too true! Jesus, other than at Christmas, is ignored and mostly forgotten by the world in which we live. It's so easy to do. Even people who claim to know Him on a personal relationship basis forget Him until life dishes up something that can't be handled without His help. In spite of knowing this, God the Heavenly Father loved this world and you and me so much that He sent His only Son to live among us and most importantly, die for us! What amazing love! So when you celebrate this Christmas, make a renewed effort not to forget the reason for this season . . . Jesus Christ!

Regarding Jesus: The ones who missed Him
were caught up in religious tradition.

(Henry Blackaby)

For God did not send his Son into the world to condemn the

world, but to save the world through him

(John 3:17).

The Star of Christmas

Back during World War II, a little boy and his daddy were driving home on Christmas Eve. They drove past rows of houses with Christmas trees and decorations in the windows. In many of the windows the little boy noticed a star. He asked his father, "Daddy, why do some of the people have a star in the window?"

His daddy said that the star meant that the family had a son in the war. As they passed the last house, suddenly the little boy caught sight of the evening star in the sky. "Look, Daddy, God must have a Son in the war too! He's got a star in His window!"[1]

Smart little boy! Yes . . . God has a Son who also went to war. The war Jesus came to wage is against sins, injustices, prejudices, traditions, and unbelief. And that war took Him all the way to a cross and a tomb from which He burst forth on Easter day in victory for you and me!

Probably the reason we all go so haywire at Christmas time with the endless unrestrained and often silly buying of gifts is that we don't quite know how to put our love into words.

(Harlan Miller)

Of the increase of his government and peace there will be no end. He will reign on David's throne and over his kingdom, establishing and upholding it with justice and righteousness from that time on and forever. The zeal of the LORD Almighty will accomplish this

(Isa. 9:7).

This will be a sign to you: You will find a baby

wrapped in cloths and lying in a manger

(Luke 2:12).

The Superhuman Saviour

Daniel Webster, while dining with some literary figures at the Christmas season, confessed his faith in Jesus Christ. A man who did not believe in the "deity" of Christ asked, "Mr. Webster, can you comprehend how Jesus Christ can be both God and man?"

He responded, "No sir, I cannot understand it. And I would be ashamed to acknowledge Christ as my Savior if I could comprehend it. He could be no greater than myself, and such is my conviction of accountability to God, my sense of sinfulness before Him, and my knowledge of my own incapability to recover myself, that I feel I need a superhuman Savior."

Exactly . . . why would anyone want to worship something that could easily be understood? This is the mystery of Christmas — how could Jesus Christ be both man and God? And I'm glad it's still a mystery. Here's where faith enters the equation. We accept this fact by faith.

Late in time behold Him come,
offspring of the virgin's womb. . . . Veiled in
flesh the godhead see; hail the incarnate deity.

(Line from the hymn, "Hark The Herald Angels Sing")

*Simeon took him in his arms and praised
God, saying: "Sovereign Lord, as you have
promised, you now dismiss your servant in
peace. For my eyes have seen your salvation,
which you have prepared in the sight of all
people, a light for revelation to the Gentiles
and for glory to your people Israel"*
(Luke 2:28–32).

It's a God

A group of first graders decided that for this pageant they would produce their very own Christmas program. They produced their own updated nativity story. All the major characters were there . . . Joseph, the shepherds, the angels, the wise men from afar . . . but where was Mary?

Shortly after the production began, there was heard some moaning and groaning coming from behind the bales of straw . . . Mary was in labor!

A first grader doctor with a white coat and black bag was ushered onto the stage and then disappeared with Joseph behind the bales of straw. After a few moments, the doctor emerged from behind the bales of straw with a jubilant smile on his face and holding a baby in his arms. With great drama in his presence, he solemnly announced in a loud voice, to the audience: "It's a GOD!"

At Christmas, the Lord prepares
a table for His children . . . but too many of
them are on a diet.

But you, Bethlehem Ephrathah, though you are

small among the clans of Judah, out of you will

come for Me one who will be ruler over Israel,

whose origins are from of old, from ancient times

(Mic. 5:2).

Voice with a Touch

Max DePree tells about his granddaughter, Zoe (Greek word for "life"), who was born prematurely and weighed only one pound, seven ounces. She was so small that Max's wedding ring would slip onto her arm and go all the way up to her shoulder. The doctors gave her very little chance of survival. The tiny child was attached to a respirator, two IV's, and a feeding tube. Zoe's biological father had abandoned his family a month prior to her birth. Max was assigned by a wise nurse to become the child's surrogate father. He was instructed to establish a daily routine of visiting his grandchild and rubbing her body with the tip of his finger. While he caressed her, he was to speak softly and lovingly to her. The nurse said it was crucial for Zoe to connect the voice with the touch. (Oh, yes, Zoe survived!)[2]

The connection of the loving touch with the voice is just what God did in sending His Son! And that's what we do as we share the Christ of Christmas with others.

To feel sorry for the needy at Christmas is not
the mark of a Christian . . . to help them is.

He will stand and shepherd his flock, in the
strength of the Lord, in the majesty of the
name of the Lord his God. And they will live securely,
for then his greatness will reach to the ends of the earth.
And he will be their peace

(Mic. 5:4–5).

It is Christmas every time you let

God love others through you . . . yes, it is

Christmas every time you smile at your brother

and offer him your hand.

(Mother Teresa of Calcutta)

Watch Out

A certain little boy desperately wanted a watch. Day after day he begged his parents for a watch. His parents didn't see the real need and tried to ignore their son's requests. The boy's obsession became so great that the father finally forbade him to say another word about the watch.

Christmas was approaching and the boy knew that his opportunity for getting a watch depended on immediate action. But he also knew that his father had forbade him from bothering them. This would take some creativity. The boy's family had a tradition of learning a Bible verse every week and reciting it for the family at the end of the week. The boy carefully considered his choice of a verse and practiced it all week. At the time of recitation, he recited his verse without a flaw: "What I say unto you I say unto you all, WATCH!"

This boy got his watch.[3]

It is the custom to sneer at the modern
apartment house, television, big city
Christmas, with its commercial taint . . .
office parties, artificial Christmas trees . . .
but future generations in search of their lost
Christmases may well remember its innocence;
yes, and its beauty, too.

(Paul Gallico)

It is written in Isaiah the prophet: "I will send my
messenger ahead of you, who will prepare your way . . . a
voice of one calling in the desert, 'Prepare the way for the
Lord, make straight paths for him' "

(Mark 1:2-3).

I Wonder Why

Curious . . . that light in the sky
    I wonder why
Curious . . . a star moving to the East
    I wonder why
Curious . . . it's pointing down to a stable
    I wonder why
Curious . . . the star is shining with glory
    I wonder why
Curious . . . I see shepherds running
    I wonder why.
Curious . . . there are kings riding camels
    I wonder why
Curious . . . my need to follow
    I wonder why
Curious . . . a babe, a manger . . . I love Him
    I wonder why

Curious . . . tears, awareness, joy, He loves me
I wonder why.[4]

The Christmas spirit brings home to us . . . or should
bring home to us . . . the profound biblical truth that "It
is more blessed to give than to receive." Anything which
inspires unselfishness makes for our ennoblement.
Christmas does that. I am all for Christmas.

(B. C. Forbes)

Give, and it will be given to you. A good measure,
pressed down, shaken together and running over, will
be poured into your lap. For with the measure you
use, it will be measured to you

(Luke 6:38).

Illegal Christmas

Did you know that there was a time when commemorating Christmas was illegal? Why? Because, supposedly, so many of its customs were pre-Christian, Christmas was forbidden in Scotland in 1583, abolished in 1647 by the Puritans, and made a penal offense in 1659.

Even mince pies were illegal in early New England. The very first Christmas pies, baked in the time of Henry VIII, were oblong instead of round, because they were supposed to represent the manger. The filling symbolized the many gifts of the Magi to the Christ child.

When images of the baby Jesus began to decorate the tops of the pies, they were outlawed.

And did you know that any kind of Christmas celebration did not become a legal act in the United States until the 19th century?!

When we were children we were grateful to
those who filled our stockings with toys at
Christmas-tide. Why are we not grateful to
God for filling our stockings with legs?

(G.K. Chesterton)

After Jesus was born in Bethlehem in Judea, during
the time of King Herod, Magi from the east
came to Jerusalem and asked, "Where is the one who has
been born king of the Jews? We saw his star in the east
and have come to worship him"

(Matt. 2:1–2).

*Many brought offerings to Jerusalem
for the LORD and valuable gifts for Hezekiah
king of Judah. From then on he was
highly regarded by all the nations*
(2 Chron. 32:23).

Christmas Emotions

In the cartoon strip, "Sally Forth," Sally says to her mother, after she has just viewed the large family Christmas tree with all the packages beneath it, "Have you ever noticed how one particular emotion gets real strong at Christmas time?"

In the next frame, her mother reflects and then answers: "I sure have, Honey. I get so nostalgic at this time of the year. I like to think back to the times of Christmas when I was your age . . . the memories of decorating the tree . . . singing carols . . . baking cookies . . . it's so much a part of the holidays for me. I'm impressed that someone your age is already aware of the richness of holiday memories."

In the last frame, Sally is by the tree, looking at the piles of wrapped gifts and thinks to herself: *Memories? I was thinking about GREED!*

I will not be responsible for anyone who does not have a Merry Christmas and a Happy New Year. Hugh Quinn.

(A notice in the *Detroit Free Press* to solve the Christmas-greeting problem for ad-man Hugh Quinn.)

In the sixth month, God sent the angel Gabriel to Nazareth, a town in Galilee, to a virgin pledged to be married to a man named Joseph, a descendant of David

(Luke 1:26–27).

Christmas Lessons for Children

When you ask me what I want and what I'm going to get, I learn that Christmas is GETTING.

When you tell me I'd better be good, I learn that Christmas is CONDITION.

When you make promises and don't keep them, I learn that Christmas is DISAPPOINTMENT.

When you are short-tempered and make threats, I learn that Christmas is UNPREDICTABLE.

When you hurry around, get up early, and stay up late, I learn that Christmas is BUSY.

When you do things for others and help me to do the same, I learn that Christmas is SHARING.

When you go to church and take me with you, I learn that Christmas is WORSHIP.

When you hum to yourself and smile at strangers, I learn that Christmas is PEACE.

When you put up lights and bake cookies, I learn that Christmas is PLEASURE.

When you stop in your busy day and spend time with me, I learn that Christmas is LOVE.[5]

I've wanted one of these
ever since I was a little girl.

(A quote from a three-year-old after ripping
into a Christmas present.)[6]

And you, my child, will be called
a prophet of the Most High; for you will go on
before the Lord to prepare the way for him
(Luke 1:76).

The First Christmas Celebration

History tells us that Christmas was first celebrated in the year A.D. 96, but it would be almost 40 years more before it was officially adopted as a Christian festival. It wasn't until the fifth century that the day of its celebration became permanently fixed on the 25th day of December.

Up to that time it had been irregularly observed at various times of the year . . . in December, in April, and in May, but most frequently in January.

You also should know that since it's been celebrated, not a single great battle of any war has been fought on any December 25! Some battles have occurred on the 24th or 26th. So the Advent of Peace on Earth has been observed by a cessation of hostilities, at least for this one day. I'm for celebrating this Christmas and every Christmas free of hostilities.

Christmas is that wonderful time of
anticipation . . . when hope becomes a shining
star, when children's wishes become prayers,
and days are x'd on calendars.

An angel of the Lord appeared to him in

a dream and said, "Joseph son of David, do not

be afraid to take Mary home as your wife, because what

is conceived in her is from the Holy Spirit"

(Matt. 1:20).

Once in the year and only once,
the whole world stands still to celebrate
the advent of a life. Only Jesus claims this
worldwide, undying remembrance.

Making Kids Happy

The manager of a large department store in the upper Midwest relates this story of a middle-aged gentleman who spends a great deal of money and time in the toy department in the two or three weeks preceding Christmas. He waits and watches for poorly dressed children. When he sees one of them looking longingly at some particular toy, he comes over to the child, takes that particular item to the cashier, buys it, has it wrapped, and presents it to the child.

He has no children of his own but he does make many little ones happy, if but for one day. These are kids who might not have anything for Christmas.

What a delightful little plan at Christmas. Think a moment. . . . Are there kids, or for that matter adults, whom you could bless in some way with your generosity this season?

Christmas is a time for patience . . . when we
try once more to mold our lives in the image
of Him whose birthday we celebrate.

She will give birth to a son, and you are to give him the

name Jesus, because he will save his people from their sins

(Matt. 1:21).

The Christmas Card

Did you know that at each Christmas about 95 percent of American families will exchange Christmas cards . . . nearly an average of 60 per family? This is a staggering four billion cards mailed during the Christmas season. Where did it all start?

Museum Director, Henry Cole, during the mid-19th century used to write short notes to friends at Christmas, wishing them a joyful holiday season. In 1843, he had no time to write all those notes so he asked his artist friend, John Horsely, to design a printed greeting card. Inadvertently, he'd just invented the Christmas card.

Quick, now . . . who is usually the person in the world with the longest Christmas card list? During most Christmas seasons, the president of the United States will send out more than 40,000 cards! I'm for an exchange of cards which is meaningful, thoughtful, and caring.

Christmas is a time for giving . . .
the wise men brought and gave their best,
but Jesus Christ showed us that the gift of self
will out-give all of the rest.

Suddenly a great company of the heavenly host

appeared with the angel, praising God and saying,

"Glory to God in the highest, and on earth

peace to men on whom his favor rests"

(Luke 2:13–14).

The Moon's Hidden Side

The distance between the earth and the moon is just about exactly 239,000 miles. It takes 27.3 days for the moon to complete one full revolution around the earth and it also takes exactly the same time for the moon to spin once on its own axis. This means that the moon remains at a standstill in relation to the earth's movement so that it always presents the same face, the same side to the earth.

With that as an introductory background . . . did you know that it was on Christmas Day of 1968 that American astronauts Frank Borman, William Anders, and James Lovell became the first men to see, with their own eyes, the hidden side of the moon? They were excited and so impressed with their first sighting that they read the creation account from the Bible, which is found in Genesis 1!

Christmas is a time for understanding others
and for making new discoveries about the
world and the people living in this world.

*In those days Caesar Augustus issued a decree
that a census should be taken of the entire
Roman world. (This was the first census that took
place while Quirinius was governor of Syria.)
And everyone went to his own town to register*
(Luke 2:1–3).

What can I give him,
Poor as I am?
If I were a shepherd
I would bring a lamb;
If I were a wise man,
I would do my part;
Yet what I can I give him —
Give my heart.

Christina Georgina Rossetti (1830–1894)

88

A Christmas Song

"What would you like for a Christmas present?" To any young girl, such a question would evoke visions of long-wished-for somethings . . . but to Dolly it was a different matter. She gave this answer to her father, John Byron, "Write me a poem."

So on Christmas morning in 1749, Dolly found on her plate at breakfast a piece of paper on which was written the poem entitled, "Christmas Day for Dolly."

Soon after, John Wainwright, organist of Manchester Church, set it to music. On the following Christmas morning, Byron and Dolly were awakened by the sound of singing below their windows. It was Wainwright and his choir singing Dolly's song, which we know today as "Christians Awake." The first line goes, "Christians awake, salute the happy morn, Where-on the Saviour of the world was born."

Christmas is a time for children
and no matter what their age . . .
spirit is their ticket
and the heart is the only gauge.

So Joseph also went up from the town of Nazareth in

Galilee to Judea, to Bethlehem the town of David, because

he belonged to the house and line of David

(Luke 2:4).

Prayer for Peace

Lord, make me an instrument of Thy peace.
Where there is hatred, let me sow love;
Where there is injury, pardon;
Where there is doubt, faith;
Where there is despair, hope;
Where there is darkness, light;
Where there is sadness, joy.

O Divine Master, grant that I may not so much
Seek to be consoled, as to console;
To be understood, as to understand;
To be loved, as to love;
For it is in giving that we receive;
It is in pardoning that we are pardoned;
And it is in dying that we are born to eternal life.

(St. Francis of Assisi)

Christmas is a time for learning . . . a time
when new truth is uncovered, and trusting
children often teach the old.

*The child's father and mother marveled at what was said
about him. Then Simeon blessed them and said to Mary,
his mother: "This child is destined to cause the falling
and rising of many in Israel, and to be a sign that will be
spoken against, so that the thoughts of many hearts will be
revealed. And a sword will pierce your own soul too"*
(Luke 2:33–35).

Silent Night

In the Austrian village of Hallein on Christmas Eve 1818, the organist Franz Gruber composed a hymn called "Song of Heaven" and played it and sang it in church the following night. A man from a nearby town happened to hear the song and, being impressed, memorized the words and music which he later taught to a traveling quartet.

By 1854 the piece had become so popular that a search was made for its unknown composer and Gruber was found. He then learned that his song had been memorized and sung for 36 years and had become the most beloved Christmas hymn of all time under another name: "SILENT NIGHT!"

At this date it meant little to Franz Gruber, who was 67 and remained an obscure and impoverished organist until his death in 1863.

Christmas is the time for sharing . . . a time to
reach out to touch the needy, with a
reach that extends to heaven, then to earth,
bringing them together.

And there were shepherds living out in the fields

nearby, keeping watch over their flocks by night.

An angel of the Lord appeared to them, and the

glory of the Lord shone around them

(Luke 2:8–9).

When Jesus spoke again to the people,
he said, "I am the light of the world.
Whoever follows me will never walk in darkness,
but will have the light of life"

(John 8:12).

Give Someone Else a Chance

Several years ago, a couple of weeks before Christmas, Mrs. Herbert Boettcher of Waterloo, Iowa, was called by a radio quiz program coming from Chicago named "Ladies Be Seated." She correctly answered the question and received a $2,000 prize.

Later in the same December, the day before Christmas, her name was again picked by the same program. When they called her, and she knew the answer, she replied, "Please call somebody else and give them a Christmas present!"

She gave up her chance, so Mrs. Gertrude Martin of Pontiac, Michigan, received $1,000 for identifying Carrie Nation as the leader of the temperance movement.

What a wonderful gesture exhibiting the spirit of Christmas . . . "give somebody else" a Christmas present. Let's keep that thought in mind during this season!

Christmas is a time for love . . . a time to
shed inhibitions, a time to show that we care,
a time to say words too long unsaid.

The shepherd returned, glorifying and

praising God for all the things they had heard

and seen, which were just as they had been told

(Luke 2:20).

The Christmas Invasion

On June 6, 1944, the greatest armed force ever assembled landed on the beaches of Normandy. The Allied Expeditionary Forces invaded enemy-held territory. There were more than 5,000 ships, 10,000 planes, and 200,000 soldiers coming against the Nazi-occupied continent. For weeks, men and supplies, heavy artillery equipment, and thousands and thousands of tons of explosives and ordnance were flown to assist the massive invasion . . . rumbling tanks, strafing fighter-bombers, and swiftly advancing armies marked that D-Day.

Contrast that to God's invasion. It was D-Day . . . the fullness of time, the turning point of human history. The world was occupied by the adversary. Humankind was imprisoned by the enemies of sin and death. The world was in the control of a network of powers hostile to God and all He stood for. The King of the universe, the Lord God Almighty, launched His invasion of planet Earth, and . . . all one could hear was the gentle breathing of a tiny baby asleep in His mother's arms.[7]

It was, oh, so easy to miss His first coming . . . and if we're not careful, we may miss Him again this year.

For the law was given through Moses; grace and truth came through Jesus Christ. No one has ever seen God, but God the One and Only, who is at the Father's side, has made him known (John 1:17–18).

Top Ten Uses for Fruitcake

10. Save it until next summer and use it as a boat anchor.

9. Take it to the office and use it for a paper weight.

8. Keep it at home and use it for a doorstop.

7. Use it as a step stool in your kitchen.

6. Let the little kids use it as a booster seat.

5. Save it for summer and use it for a flower press.

4. Carry it in your trunk to use in emergencies for a tire block.

3. Put it in your workshop and use it for an anvil.

2. Save it until next year and use it as a Yule log.

1. Save it until next year and give it back to the person who
   gave it to you.

Friends don't give friends fruitcake.
(Seen on a bumper sticker)

Through him all things were made; without him nothing was made that has been made. In him was life, and that life was the light of men. The light shines in the darkness, but the darkness has not understood it

(John 1:3-5).

The Christ child stood at Mary's knee,
His hair was like a crown,
And all the flowers looked up at Him,
And all the stars looked down.

G. K. Chesterton (1874–1936)

Directive From the
"Know-it-all" Department in Washington

This year, only inoffensive nativity pageants will be allowed:

There shall be no mention of Mary riding a donkey. Unfair to animals.

No reference to innkeeper allowed so as not to cast aspersions on hospitality industries.

No swaddling clothes which is a clear sign of child abuse.

There will be an equal number of boy shepherds and girl shepherds.

No reference shall be made to seeing a star so as not to offend people living in smog.

Any and all gifts shall be wrapped in recycled paper and recycled ribbons.

King Herod shall be accompanied by Queen Herod and speak half the dialogue.

There shall be at least three Wise Persons of appropriate ethnic and gender mix.

When the family leaves for Egypt, Joseph shall carry the baby and Mary the luggage.

Since religious observances should unite rather than divide, there shall be no "Gloria in excelsis Deo" nor any "Merry Christmases." A simple "Season's Greetings" is preferable.

Christmas is real . . .
it's the rest of the year that's pretend.

John replied in the words of Isaiah the prophet,
"I am the voice of one calling in the desert,
'Make straight the way for the Lord' "
(John 1:23).

First, Last, and Always

The Old Testament cries: BEHOLD, HE COMES!

The Gospels declare: BEHOLD, HE IS BORN!

Then they declare: BEHOLD, HE DIES!

Acts declares: BEHOLD, HE LIVES!

The Epistles join in with, BEHOLD, HE SAVES!

The Apocalypse finalizes with the Hallelujah chorus:

> BEHOLD, HE REIGNS!

It is JESUS . . .

> first,
>> last,
>>> and all the way through!

(J. Sidlow Baxter)

Somehow, folks keep trying to steal the joy
and wonder of this special season.

The next day John saw Jesus coming toward him

and said, "Look, the Lamb of God, who

takes away the sin of the world!"

(John 1:29).

It Was That Night

It was that ethereal night

when a matchless star stood glowing in the East,

trailing a man, a woman, a burdened beast.

    It was that incredible night

    when an innkeeper became the first to say:

    "I have no room for You this day."

        It was that incomparable night

        when Gabriel came ecstatic to the earth,

        proclaiming glad tidings of a royal birth.

It was that immortal night

when a caring God reached gently down to lay,

His supreme gift, Love, upon the hay.

(Fred Bauer)

Christmas is the time to remember timeless
stories from days of old, a time to ponder
what's ahead and a time to open another door.

When Joseph and Mary had done everything required by the

Law of the Lord, they returned to Galilee to their own town

of Nazareth. And the child grew and became strong; he was

filled with wisdom and the grace of God was upon him

(Luke 2:39–40).

For the customs of the peoples are worthless;
they cut a tree out of the forest, and a
craftsman shapes it with his chisel. They adorn
it with silver and gold; they fasten it with
hammer and nails so it will not totter
(Jer. 10:3–4).

Not Another Word

Thomas Aquinas (born 1225) has created what is considered the single greatest intellectual achievement of Western civilization in his "Summa Theological." It contained 38 treatises, 3,000 articles, and 3,000 objections. Rejecting the traditional Platonist views and drawing a sharp distinction between reason and faith, he attempted to gather into one coherent whole all known truth. Anthropology, ethics, physics, astronomy, political and military theory, and philosophy all organized under the "Doctrine of God."

On December 6, 1273, while at worship, he "received a glimpse of Glory." Suddenly he knew his attempt to describe God fell so short, he never picked up his pen again. His writings ceased. His secretary Reginald encouraged him to carry on. Thomas replied. "I can do no more. Such things have been revealed to me that all I have written is as so much straw." He never wrote another word and died a year later.

What's the point? The danger of Christmas is that you might see God and be changed.[8]

As man alone, Jesus could not have saved us,
as God alone, He would not.
Incarnate, He could and did.

(Malcolm Muggeridge)

I have seen and I testify that this is the Son of God
(John 1:34).

What a Way to Live

A young man felt that God had called him to the foreign mission field. In the back of his Bible he wrote two words and underlined them: NO RESERVES. Later, after turning down some rather high paying jobs, he wrote these two words and underlined them: NO RETREATS.

Completing his seminary training he went to the mission field. However, too soon, he was stricken with a disease and died in a few weeks. At his funeral, the pastor read from the back of his Bible his words: NO RESERVES. NO RETREATS. And then read his last words penned by him while he was laying on his hospital bed: NO REGRETS.

We are approaching another NEW YEAR. . . . What are you living for? What is the goal of your life? Do you really want to make a difference in God's world?

Some people count the quality of life by days lived; others by failures mastered; but the final determination is when you stand before your Maker. Will you be able to say: NO RESERVES. NO RETREATS. NO REGRETS!

Many Americans no longer celebrate the *arrival* of the new year, they celebrate the *survival* of the old year.
(Andy Hall)

But one thing I do: Forgetting what is behind
and straining toward what is ahead, I press on
toward the goal to win the prize for which God has
called me heavenward in Christ Jesus
(Phil. 3:13–14).

The holiest of all holidays are those kept by

ourselves in silence and apart:

the secret anniversaries of the heart.

Henry Wadsworth Longfellow (1807–1882)

The Christmas Spirit

I AM THE CHRISTMAS SPIRIT!

I enter the homes of poverty, causing pale-faced children to open their hearts in wonder.

I cause the miser's clutched hand to relax and paint a bright spot on his/her soul.

I cause the aged to renew their youth.

I keep romance alive in the heart of children.

I cause eager feet to climb dark stairways with filled baskets, leaving others happy.

I cause the prodigal to pause on the wild, wasteful way to think about a token of love.

I come softly to the house of pain.

In a thousand ways I cause the weary world to look up into the face of God.

I AM THE CHRISTMAS SPIRIT!

The challenge for us today is to hear
the Christmas story as if we were
hearing it for the first time.

What is more, I consider everything a loss compared to
the surpassing greatness of knowing Christ Jesus my
Lord, for whose sake I have lost all things. I consider them
rubbish, that I may gain Christ and be found in him
(Phil. 3:8–9).

Ten Commandments for Christmas

1. THOU SHALT remember to keep Christ in Christmas.

2. THOU SHALT pause in thy busyness to consider the magnitude of God's gift to mankind.

3. THOU SHALT remember that Mary and Joseph found no room in the inn. Give Christ room in your heart.

4. THOU SHALT participate in the Christmas activities prepared by your church.

5. THOU SHALT be of a generous heart in answering the appeals of your church at Christmas.

6. THOU SHALT take time to plan for the happiness of those outside your family circle.

7. THOU SHALT enjoy, in unhurried calm, the heritage of Christmas carols and Christmas art.

8. THOU SHALT give of thyself in all thy gifts, for giving is not a duty but a joy in sharing.

9. THOU SHALT remember with patience all who serve you this holiday season.

10. THOU SHALT teach the children the true message of Christmas, of the Prince of Peace.

Think . . . today, if you toss out one of
those musical Christmas cards, you are
throwing away more computer power than
existed in the entire world in 1950.

I can do everything through him who gives me strength
(Phil. 4:13).

Notes

1 *Parables, Etc.*, 12/83.

2 Max DePree, *Leadership Jazz* (New York, NY: Dell Publishing, Inc., 1992).

3 Donald Wildmon, editor, *American Family Association Newsletter*.

4 Jeanne Ervin, *The Pastor's Story File,* 12/94.

5 Adapted from Katharine Kersey's column, *Raising Children*.

6 *Country*, April/May 1989.

7 Jon H. Allen, *Illustration Digest*, Num. 4, 1995.

8 Allen, *Illustration Digest.*

If you enjoyed this book we also have available:

Mini-Moments for Fathers

Mini-Moments for Graduates

Mini-Moments for Leaders

Mini-Moments for Mothers

Mini-Moments with Angels

At Christian bookstores nationwide